7/16

MAKING THE PLAY

SOCCER

BY VALERIE BODDEN

CREATIVE EDUCATION • CREATIVE PAPERBACKS

Published by Creative Education and Creative Paperbacks
P.O. Box 227, Mankato, Minnesota 56002
Creative Education and Creative Paperbacks
are imprints of The Creative Company
www.thecreativecompany.us

Design and production by The Design Lab
Art direction by Rita Marshall
Printed in the United States of America

Photographs by Dreamstime (Amy S. Myers), iStockphoto
(t_kimura), photosinbox.com, Shutterstock (Bplanet,
EKS, HSNphotography, In Green, Ralf Juergen Kraft,
matimix, Mega Pixel, Sergey Nivens, ostill, Tungphoto)

Library of Congress Cataloging-in-Publication Data
Bodden, Valerie.
Soccer / Valerie Bodden.
p. cm. — (Making the play)
Includes index.
Summary: An elementary introduction to the physics involved
in the sport of soccer, including scientific concepts such as
spin and friction, and actions such as dribbling and kicking.
ISBN 978-1-60818-657-0 (hardcover)
ISBN 978-1-62832-236-1 (pbk)
ISBN 978-1-56660-688-2 (eBook)
1. Soccer—Juvenile literature. 2. Physics—Juvenile literature. I. Title.

GV943.25.B64 2016
796.334—dc23   2015007572

CCSS: RI.1.1, 2, 3, 4, 5, 6, 7; RI.2.1, 2, 3, 5, 6, 7,
10; RI.3.1, 3, 5, 7, 8; RF.2.3, 4; RF.3.3

First Edition HC 9 8 7 6 5 4 3 2 1
First Edition PBK 9 8 7 6 5 4 3 2 1

CONTENTS

SOCCER AND SCIENCE 4

SPIN 8

FORCE AND FRICTION 14

ACTIVITY: FRICTION ON THE MOVE 20

GLOSSARY 22

READ MORE 23

WEBSITES 23

INDEX 24

SOCCER AND SCIENCE

You **dribble** the soccer ball as you run down the field. Suddenly, you pull your leg back and kick. Goal!

GOAL!

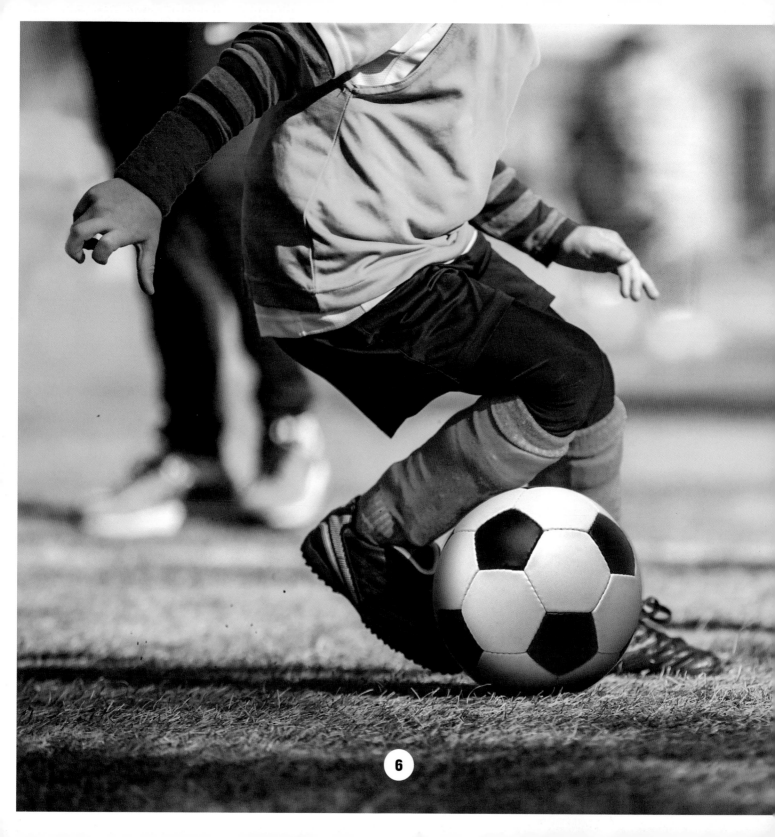

Do you think about science when you play soccer? Probably not. But you use science anyway. A science called physics (*FIZ-icks*) can help you dribble, kick, and score. Let's see how!

SPIN

Soccer players can make the ball "bend." This means that the ball curves while in the air. How do they do it?

SPIN IT

Kick the ball off-center instead of in the middle.

To bend, the ball needs spin. A ball with spin turns around its center.

It moves forward at the same time.

Spin makes air flow faster past one side of the ball than the other.

You can put spin on a ball by kicking it off-center. Baseball pitchers use spin to throw **curveballs**, too.

MAGNUS EFFECT

Magnus force

Air flows faster past one side of the ball. This makes the ball curve.

FORCE AND FRICTION

A soccer ball on the field is at rest.

It will stay put until a **force** acts on

it. That force could be a player. Or it

could be **friction**.

INERTIA

An object at rest will stay at rest until a force acts on it.

FRICTION

MOTION

FRICTION

You can feel friction if you rub your hands together. There is friction between the ball and the grass. The ball slows down. Then it stops.

Friction helps your shoes grip the ground as you run down the field. Where else can you see friction in soccer? How about when you trap the ball? Give it a try, and make the play!

19

FRICTION ON THE MOVE

Different materials produce different amounts of friction.

WHAT YOU NEED

- Playground slide (or a board propped against a chair to make a ramp)
- Stopwatch
- Toy car and block
- Dress shoe
- Tennis shoe

WHAT YOU DO

One by one, set each object at the top of the slide. Time how long it takes the object to reach the bottom. Which object travels down the slide fastest? Do any of the objects get stuck? How can you tell if an object produces a lot of friction? What do you notice about the objects that produce the most friction?

GLOSSARY

curveballs-baseball pitches that have strong topspin to make them drop and curve

dribble-to move the soccer ball forward with repeated small kicks

force-a push or a pull

friction-a force that tries to stop two objects that are rubbing together from moving

READ MORE

Gifford, Clive. *Soccer*. Mankato, Minn.: Sea-to-Sea, 2009.

Gore, Bryson. *Physics*. Mankato, Minn.: Stargazer, 2009.

Walton, Ruth. *Let's Go to the Playground*.
Mankato, Minn.: Sea-to-Sea, 2013.

WEBSITES

DragonflyTV: Soccer
http://pbskids.org/dragonflytv/show/soccerball.html
Watch this video to learn more about the science of kicking a soccer ball.

YouTube: The Physics Behind a Curveball—The Magnus Effect
https://www.youtube.com/watch?v=YIPO3WO8IHw
Check out this video to see a soccer player bend the ball.

NOTE: Every effort has been made to ensure that the websites listed above are suitable for children, that they have educational value, and that they contain no inappropriate material. However, because of the nature of the Internet, it is impossible to guarantee that these sites will remain active indefinitely or that their contents will not be altered.

INDEX

airflow 11

balls 4, 8, 11, 12, 14, 17, 18

bending 8, 11

dribbling 4, 7

forces 14

friction 14, 17, 18

kicking 4, 7, 12

physics 7

scoring 4, 7

spin 11, 12

trapping 18